Book 1
Excel Shortcuts
BY SAM KEY

&

Book 2
JavaScript Professional
Programming Made Easy
BY SAM KEY

Book 1
Excel Shortcuts

BY SAM KEY

The 100 Top Best Powerful Excel Keyboard Shortcuts in 1 Day!

Programming Box Set #70: Excel Shortcuts & JavaScript Professional Programming Made Easy

Table Of Contents

Introduction

I want to thank you and congratulate you for purchasing the book, "The Power of Excel Shortcuts: The 100 Top Best Powerful Excel Keyboard Shortcuts in 1 Day!".

This book contains proven steps and strategies on how to master the Microsoft Excel through just 100 keyboard shortcuts! However, most people will ask, "Why do you need to learn these shortcuts anyway?"

Advantages of Using Microsoft Excel

Microsoft Excel has become one of the most commonly used enterprise software in schools and offices. Its way of presenting data, which is through a spreadsheet, has helped a lot of people especially in the field of data mining. If you were going to put numerous rows of data, in let's say, a word processing program, it might take a lot of time creating tables and formatting each of them to fit in the pages. With the Microsoft Excel, these manual tasks are now much easier.

What does the Microsoft Excel have that other programs don't? For one, it has a built-in spreadsheet that you can manipulate the size and formatting. This versatile way of maneuvering the spreadsheet made it indispensable for many. Now, gone are the days were people have to manually draw tables in sheets of paper. Excel has already the tables prepared for them.

Another nifty feature of this software is its calculation function. Excel houses a myriad of formulas for solving arithmetic, financial and logical problems, among others. Thus, one doesn't even need to calculate every sum or average of a data series. Just by using a formula in Excel, everything can be done in an instant.

The Secret behind Mastering Excel

Programming Box Set #70: Excel Shortcuts & JavaScript Professional Programming Made Easy

Speaking of instant, did you know that Excel has more than a hundred keyboard shortcuts? What does this mean to you as an Excel user? It means you can continuously work on your Excel spreadsheet without having to depend on your mouse constantly for Excel functions.

This is especially helpful whenever you are inputting a lot of data, and doing this will be more efficient if both of your hands weren't switching from keyboard to mouse and vice versa, every once in a while. In addition, if your mouse suddenly chose the most inopportune time to malfunction, learning Excel shortcuts can save you from major headaches.

As such, this book will provide you 100 keyboard shortcuts which you can use in Excel. In addition, as a bonus, you will learn about alternatives in case you forget any of these shortcuts.

Thanks again for purchasing this book, I hope you enjoy it!

Chapter 1: Moving Around the Excel Screen

People typically use the mouse for navigating the Excel screen. With this device, you can manipulate every cell in Excel, including its formatting and color. Since the mouse can access the major functions in Excel through the ribbon, there is no need for you to manually-type every formula or command.

However, the only difficult thing that you cannot do with a mouse is entering text. If you're going to use an on-screen keyboard, keying in the data in every cell would probably take you a lot longer than just using the keyboard for the text.

Thus, if you're going to use the keyboard most of the time, especially if you're just starting to build the spreadsheet data from scratch, it would be helpful to learn the basic keyboard shortcuts for moving around the Excel spreadsheet.

Shortcut #1: Arrow Keys

There are four arrow keys found in the right side of your main keyboard keys. These are the Arrow Left, Arrow Right, Arrow Up, and Arrow Down keys. Intuitively, you know that you can use these keys for moving within the spreadsheet. For instance, by selecting a cell then pressing Arrow Up, it will situate the cursor in the cell directly above your selected cell.

Shortcut #2: Ctrl + Arrow Key

Let's assume that you have a block of Excel data that spans more than 50,000 rows and more than 200 columns. You would probably have a hard time using a mouse in skimming these voluminous data. As such, you can use the Ctrl + Arrow key to navigate each "ends" of the data easily. In this example, click any cell in the block of data then press Ctrl + Arrow Down. You will be immediately located to the bottom cell in that specific column.

Shortcut #3: Shift + Arrow Key

You have selected all the items in the row but you forgot to include one cell. What would you do if you needed to include the next cell in the selection? Simply press Shift + Arrow Key, where the arrow pertains to the direction of the region you want to highlight.

Shortcut #4: Ctrl + Shift + Arrow Key

The above shortcut only includes one cell in the selection; but what would happen if you want to include everything until the last cell containing a data? You then use the Ctrl + Shift + Arrow Key.

Shortcut #5: Backspace

The Backspace key immediately deletes the contents of the active cell. However, if the cell is in Edit mode, it will only delete one character in the left of the insertion point, or the blinking cursor in the Formula bar.

Shortcut #6: Delete

This key has the same function as the Backspace key. However, instead of the left side, it removes a character in the right hand side of the insertion point.

Shortcut #7: End

Pressing the End key will enable the End Mode in Excel. In this mode, if you press an Arrow key, it will directly take you to the last used cell (or if none, last cell) in that specific direction. However, if the Scroll Lock is on, pressing the End key will only take you to the lower right corner of your Excel screen.

Shortcut #8: Ctrl + End

It works the same as the End key where pressing this combination will take you to the last used cell. However, if no cells were used, it will not move to the end of the worksheet like the End key does. Also, if the insertion point is located in the Formula bar (e.g., after the first character), Ctrl + End will put this cursor at the end of the field.

Shortcut #9: Ctrl + Shift + End

This keyboard shortcut can do two functions. First, in the Formula bar, it will select every character at the right of the insertion point. On the other hand, if you use it in the worksheet, it will highlight the cells starting from the active cell (or selected cell) until the last used cell in the worksheet.

Shortcut #10: Spacebar

Aside from putting a space in your text, it can also either select or clear a checkbox.

Shortcut #11: Ctrl + Spacebar

This will select the whole column to where the active cell is located.

Shortcut #12: Shift + Spacebar

It has the same function as the above, but this shortcut selects rows instead of columns.

Shortcut #13: Ctrl + Shift + Spacebar

Pressing these keys will select your entire worksheet.

Shortcut #14: Enter

Programming Box Set #70: Excel Shortcuts & JavaScript Professional Programming Made Easy

After you have entered a data in a cell, pressing the Enter key will complete the input of data. Besides that, you can also directly go one cell below through this key. Considered as the most commonly used shortcut in Excel, you will be using the Enter key quite a lot because all Excel functions need it.

Shortcut #15: Shift + Enter

If you press Enter, you will go down one cell. Conversely, a Shift + Enter will complete an entry in a cell but the cursor will go directly above your entry.

Shortcut #16: Ctrl + Enter

Since this is a spreadsheet, it follows that after you have put an entry, you will enter another data below it. That is the common task whenever you're working on a table or database, which explains why the Enter key goes down. However, if you think that you need the downward movement, you can try Ctrl + Enter. This will plainly enter your data in the cell and it won't move your cursor to another direction.

Shortcut #17: Alt + Enter

You want the data to go into the next line in the same cell. However, if you press Enter, the cursor just moves on to the next cell in line. Pressing the Tab key doesn't work either. So what will you do? Try Alt + Enter key and see if it works.

Shortcut #18: Esc Key

The Escape key, or simply "Esc", performs a lot of nifty functions in Excel. Among of which are the following: 1) deletes a whole data in a cell, 2) exits you from a dialog box, and 3) escapes you from the full screen mode of Excel.

Programming Box Set #70: Excel Shortcuts & JavaScript Professional Programming Made Easy

Shortcut #19: Home Key

The Home key will take you to the first cell in the specific row of your active cell. However, if the Scroll Lock is on, the cursor will go to the upper-left corner of your current window.

Shortcut #20: Ctrl + Home

This shortcut, also known as the "True Home key", brings the user to the beginning of the worksheet.

Shortcut #21: Ctrl + Shift + Home

This will select all cells from the active cell up to the first cell in the worksheet.

Shortcut #22: Page Down

Scouring among rows and rows of worksheets is now easy because of this button. This will display the next page in your Excel window.

Shortcut #23: Alt + Page Down

Unlike Page Down, the Alt + Page Down combination will show the next page to the right of your current window.

Shortcut #24: Ctrl + Page Down

Flipping in several worksheets is now easy thanks to Ctrl + Page Down. This will automatically turn you over to the next worksheet.

Shortcut #25: Ctrl + Shift + Page Down

The normal way of selecting several worksheets at once is to hold Ctrl while clicking each of the worksheets to be included in the selection.

However, for those who don't think this is the practical way to do it, here's an alternative. Use the Ctrl + Shift + Page Down; it will automatically select the sheets for you.

Shortcut #26: Page Up

This is quite similar to Shortcut #22: Page Down key, except for the fact that this one goes in the opposite direction (which is upward).

Shortcut #27: Alt + Page Up

The Alt + Page Up will move your screen to the left, instead of right as what was described in Shortcut #23: Alt + Page Down.

Shortcut #28: Ctrl + Page Up

Same as Shortcut #24: Ctrl + Page Down, this will enable you to change sheets easily. However, this one goes in a counterclockwise direction.

Shortcut #29: Ctrl + Shift + Page Up

Selecting sheets is also a function of the Ctrl + Shift + Page Up. However, it will select the worksheets on the left hand side of your current sheet first.

Shortcut #30: Tab Key

Using the Tab key will enable you to move to the right hand side of the cell. Also, if you have a protected worksheet, pressing this can immediately take you to the next unlocked cell. Lastly, in case there is a dialog box, you can easily move along the options through the Tab key.

Shortcut #31: Shift + Tab

The Shift + Tab works the opposite way; if pressing Tab will take you to the right hand cell, this shortcut will locate the left cell for you. It also applies to the other functions of the Tab key. In a dialog box for instance, keying in Shift + Tab will move you to the previous option.

Shortcut #32: Ctrl + Tab

You're now done with shortcuts for moving around cells and worksheets. As such, the succeeding shortcuts in this chapter will focus on dialog boxes. For this shortcut, use it if you want to go to the next tab in a dialog box.

Shortcut #33: Ctrl + Shift + Tab

However, if you wish to go back to the previous tab in a dialog box, using the Ctrl + Shift + Tab is the right combination.

So there you have it, the first 33 keyboard shortcuts in Excel. Hopefully, through these tips you can know traverse in your multitude of cells and worksheets with no difficulty at all.

Chapter 2: Navigating the Excel Ribbon

Microsoft created the "ribbon" as a replacement to the expanding menus in the earlier versions of Microsoft Excel. It houses all the functions in Excel such as formatting, page layout, pictures, and shapes. However, since its interface is not in an expanding menu style, people are not that familiar with its keyboard shortcuts as compared to before where you can immediately see which shortcut runs which.

To help you with that, here are some of the most commonly used keyboard shortcuts for exploring the Ribbon.

Shortcut #34: Alt Key

Letters and numbers will appear in the ribbon once you push the Alt key. What happens is that it activates the access keys, wherein typing in corresponding letter or number will let you select a specific function in the ribbon.

Shortcut #35: F10

This key has the same function as the Alt key, only that pressing the F10 would require you to use your right hand instead.

Shortcut #36: Alt + Arrow Left/Right

To be able to navigate to the other tabs, use these keys.

Shortcut #37: F10 + Arrow Left/Right

Since it was previously mentioned that the F10 behaves the same way as the Alt key, pressing F10 followed by an arrow to the left or to the right will also transfer you to other tabs.

Programming Box Set #70: Excel Shortcuts & JavaScript Professional Programming Made Easy

Shortcut #38: Ctrl + F1

There's no doubt that the ribbon indeed takes up quite a lot of space in your screen. Therefore, for those who want more area for their spreadsheet, hiding the ribbon is the best option. To do that, simply press Ctrl + F1. To show the ribbon again, also press the same shortcut.

Shortcut #39: Shift + F10

Shift + F10 is similar to the right click button of your mouse. It can open menus and other options depending on where your cursor is.

Shortcut #40: F6

You can move along three areas of the screen through this key. The F6 key, will take you either to the ribbon, the spreadsheet, or the status bar.

Shortcut #41: F10 + Tab

In a tab, you can browse through the functions by pressing this combination continuously. You can also press this shortcut first, and then proceed with the arrow keys for navigation.

Shortcut #42: F10 + Shift + Tab

The above shortcut goes around the functions in a clockwise manner. On the contrary, the F10 + Shift + Tab shortcut does otherwise.

Shortcut #43: F1

In the upper right corner of the ribbon, there is a blue question mark icon. Accessing this icon will take you to the Microsoft Excel Help task pane. Alternatively, if you press F1 the same pane will open.

Since the area around the ribbon is limited, it is only appropriate that there would be less keyboard shortcuts dedicated for it. All in all, there are ten button combinations for the ribbon.

Chapter 3: Formatting the Excel Spreadsheet

If you're also a user of the Microsoft Word, you are probably familiar with formatting keyboard shortcuts such as Ctrl + B, which stands for bold text or Ctrl + I, which italicizes your text. Since you can do almost every basic feature that you need in the Word application through the keyboard, this makes the formatting easier for you.

Fortunately, even though Excel is not a word-processing program, it also has dedicated keyboard shortcuts that for formatting. These are as follows:

Shortcut #44: Alt + '

By going to the Styles group in the Home tab, you can quickly change the appearance of the cell by selecting any of the pre-installed styles in Excel. To see the formatting changes done within a cell, you click on the New Style option, which will take you to the Style dialog box. Similarly, clicking Alt + ' will get you in the same menu.

Shortcut #45: Ctrl + B

Like in Microsoft Word, Ctrl + B will either apply or remove a bold format in a text.

Shortcut #46: Ctrl + 2

This shortcut can also make the selected text into a bold type.

Shortcut #47: Ctrl + I

Letter I stands for Italics. As such, clicking Ctrl + I will turn any text into an italicized type.

Shortcut #48: Ctrl + 3

This also functions like the Ctrl + I shortcut.

Shortcut #49: Ctrl + U

Ctrl + U will put an underline in the selected text.

Shortcut #50: Ctrl + 4

Another alternative for the Ctrl +U is the Ctrl + 4 shortcut.

Shortcut #51: Ctrl + 5

To easily put a strikethrough in your text, press Ctrl + 5.

Shortcut #52: Ctrl + Shift + F

If you want more font formatting options, you can just proceed to the Font tab of the Format cells dialog box. Right-clicking a cell then selecting Format Cells will get you there, or you can just use this shortcut.

Shortcut #53: Ctrl + Shift + P

This shortcut works the same as the above.

Shortcut #54: Ctrl + Shift + &

Now that you're done with editing the text, this shortcut as well as the succeeding ones will pertain to cell formatting. As for Ctrl + Shift + &, it will put a plain black border on all sides of the cell.

Shortcut #55: Ctrl + Shift + _

On the contrary, Ctrl + Shift + _ will remove the borders that you have made.

Shortcut #56: F4

Instead of manually doing all the formatting for a number of cells, Excel has a shortcut wherein you can redo the formatting that you just did in another cell. This is the F4 function key. For example, if you have put borders in Cell A1, selecting Cell A2 then pressing F4 will also create borders for that specific cell.

Shortcut #57: Ctrl + 1

Pressing the Ctrl + 1 will show the Format Cells dialog box. In this box, you can edit every possible formatting for a cell such as number format, alignment, font, border, and fill.

The previous chapters have discussed how certain shortcuts can perform specific functions in Excel such as formatting cells and navigating the spreadsheet. In the following chapters, the topics will be about the different uses of specific buttons such as the Function keys and the Control key.

Chapter 4: Working with Function Keys

The first row of keys in your keyboard contains the function keys, which is denoted by the letter F followed by a number. In the Windows desktop, these function keys can do a variety of tasks such as adjusting the screen brightness or minimizing the volume.

Excel uses the function keys for different purposes. Thus, most people usually have a difficulty mastering the Function key shortcuts in Excel.

Shortcut #58: Alt + F1

Alt + F1 will automatically create a chart for you. Just select the range of cells containing your chart data then press this shortcut. Afterwards, a column chart will appear in the worksheet.

Shortcut #59: Alt + Shift + F1

The normal way in creating a new worksheet is by right-clicking any of the existing worksheets then choosing Insert. The same task can be done by this shortcut.

Shortcut #60: F2

In editing a formula, you can't just simply select an active cell; you have to click on the Formula bar so that you can make changes to it. Fortunately, the F2 will put the cell in Edit mode. Thus, if you want to amend a cell, there's no need for you to click on the Formula bar; just use F2 instead.

Shortcut #61: Shift + F2

The Shift + F2 shortcut will insert comments in the active cell.

Programming Box Set #70: Excel Shortcuts & JavaScript Professional Programming Made Easy

Shortcut #62: Ctrl + F2

Unlike the previous F2 combinations, this one has nothing to do with editing a cell. When you press Ctrl + F2, you will be forwarded to the Print Preview screen. Upon exiting this screen, your spreadsheet will show dotted lines which serves as a marker for a page border.

Shortcut #63: F3

Instead of constantly referring to a range of cells by their cell location (e.g., A1:D1), you can just define a name for this range. Thus, whenever you want to pertain to that specific range in a formula, you can simply put its name; there's no need for you to put the cell range. F3 will take you to the Paste Name dialog box, wherein you can list all the names created in a worksheet and their respective cell references.

Shortcut #64: Ctrl + F3

To create a new name, go to the Name Manager through Ctrl + F3.

Shortcut #65: Shift + F3

Using formulas is the heart of Microsoft Excel. Without it, you cannot do any calculations in the spreadsheet. As such, there is a dedicated tab for Formulas in the Excel ribbon. However, it may take quite a lot of time for users to efficiently look for the appropriate formula with all the possible options in the Formulas tab. Because of this, the Shift + F3 key combination is made. It opens the Insert Function dialog box, wherein you can easily search for a formula by just typing in the description of what you need to do.

Shortcut #66: Ctrl + F4

You don't need to click that "X" mark in the upper left corner of your Excel screen just to close the application; a simple Ctrl + F4 is enough to do the job.

Shortcut #67: F5

Rummaging through a lot of cells takes a lot of work, especially if you're dealing with thousands of rows in a spreadsheet. The Go To dialog box, which can be accessed through F5, will help you reach that specific cell or range that you wanted to see.

Shortcut #68: Ctrl + F5

By default, all workbooks are always in full screen mode in Excel. However, if you're doing work on several Excel files at once, it may be hard to switch from one file to the other when each workbook is on full screen. Through Ctrl + F5, the selected file restore to window size in the Excel screen so that you can easily switch across files.

Shortcut #69: Shift + F6

This works the same as Shortcut #40: F6, albeit in a counterclockwise direction.

Shortcut #70: Ctrl + F6

If you have more than one workbook open, pressing Ctrl + F6 will let you switch among these workbooks.

Shortcut #71: F7

Aside from Microsoft Word, the Excel application has also a built-in spell checker. To check the spelling of every word in your spreadsheet, press F7. This will run the Spelling dialog box. Apart from detecting erroneous spellings, it also suggests possible words that can replace the incorrect word.

Shortcut #72: Ctrl + F7

As mentioned before, you should not use the full screen mode when working with several Excel files. This is so that you can select each workbook with ease. The Ctrl + F7 shortcut executes the Move command so that you can drag the unneeded workbooks in another area in the Excel screen where it can't obstruct your view.

Shortcut #73: F8

Upon pressing F8, the Excel goes into an Extend Selection mode. This enables you to use the arrow keys to extend the current selection. Pressing the same key will also lift the Extend Selection mode.

Shortcut #74: Shift + F8

The limitation of the F8 key is that it only adds adjacent cells in the selection. Through Shift + F8, you can now add any nonadjacent cell by using arrow keys.

Shortcut #75: Ctrl + F8

To resize your workbook, use Ctrl + F8. This will run the Size command for workbooks that are not in a full screen mode.

Shortcut #76: Alt + F8

A macro is a set of actions created using the Visual Basic programming language. What it does is to automate a set of tasks in Excel. For example, you're going to retrieve a data in a one sheet then you'll paste the said data in another sheet. However, if you're going to do the copy-paste task for thousands of data, it might take you a long time. As such, you can use the macro for this. Alt + F8 will open the Macro dialog box, where you can record and run a macro.

Shortcut #77: F9

This is the Refresh button in Excel. Once you refresh a workbook, it will recalculate all new formulas in the said file.

Shortcut #78: Shift + F9

On the other hand, Shift + F9 will only recalculate the formulas in the worksheet you are currently working on.

Shortcut #79: Ctrl + Alt + F9

This has the same function as F9, but it will also recalculate formulas that have not been changed.

Shortcut #80: Ctrl + Alt + Shift + F9

Aside from doing what the Ctrl + Alt + F9 shortcut does, it also rechecks all dependent formulas for any errors.

Shortcut #81: Alt + Shift + F10

Smart tags are data that are labeled in a particular type. For instance, a person's name in an Outlook email message can be labeled with this tag. You can open the smart tag menu through this shortcut.

Shortcut #82: Ctrl + F10

This will enable a workbook to display in full screen mode (or maximized mode).

Shortcut #83: F11

The Shortcut #58: Alt + F1 will let you create charts by highlighting the data series. Similarly, the F11 key has the same function except that you don't need to select the data series; it will automatically detect the data for you. Another difference between these two shortcuts is that the Alt + F1 will display the chart in the same worksheet, while the F1 key will make another worksheet for the new chart.

Shortcut #84: Shift + F11

This is an alternative to Shortcut #59: Alt + Shift + F1, wherein it will insert a new worksheet.

Shortcut #85: Alt + F11

Alt + F11 will open the Microsoft Visual Basic Editor. In this menu, you can create or edit a macro by using the Visual Basic for Applications (VBA) programming language.

Shortcut #86: F12

The F12 key is the shortcut for the Save As dialog box. It lets you save your Excel file among the available formats.

In case you're wondering why the F1, F4, F6 and F10 keys as well as some of their derivatives are not included in the list, these function keys have already been discussed in the previous chapters. Moreover, as this book specifically claims that it will contain at least a hundred keyboard shortcuts, putting these function keys again in the list will not create an accurate count of all the shortcuts.

Chapter 5: Discovering Ctrl Combinations

There are more than 50 Ctrl key combinations that you can use in the Excel sheet, with some shortcuts comprising of special characters instead of the usual alphanumeric ones. Thus, it would be unpractical to include every possible shortcut, especially if there's a little chance that a typical user will use them all.

With these reasons, only the f14 most valuable Ctrl shortcuts will be contained in the list below.

Shortcut #87: Ctrl + ;

Ctrl + ; will show the current date in the active cell.

Shortcut #88: Ctrl + Shift + #

Ctrl + Shift + # will change the date into a day-month-year format.

Shortcut #89: Ctrl + A

This is an alternative to Shortcut #13: Ctrl + Shift + Spacebar. Pressing these keys will also select the whole worksheet.

Shortcut #90: Ctrl + C

Ctrl + C will copy the contents of the active cell.

Shortcut #91: Ctrl + F

If you need to search for a specific data, you don't have to go to the Home tab and choose Find & Select. By pressing Ctrl + F, you can now access the Find and Replace dialog box immediately.

Programming Box Set #70: Excel Shortcuts & JavaScript Professional Programming Made Easy

Shortcut #92: Ctrl + K

To insert or edit a hyperlink, use this shortcut.

Shortcut #93: Ctrl + R

This activates the Fill Right command. To use this, simply click on a cell you want filled then press Ctrl + R. It will copy all the formatting and contents of the cell to its left.

Shortcut #94: Ctrl + S

Ctrl + S will automatically save your file in its current name, location and format.

Shortcut #95: Ctrl + V

After doing Shortcut #90: Ctrl + C, you then proceed with Ctrl + V to paste the contents that you have copied.

Shortcut #96: Ctrl + Alt + V

Since the above shortcut will paste all the data as is, the Ctrl + Alt + V will give you most pasting options as it will open the Paste Special dialog box.

Shortcut #97: Ctrl + W

This combination is an alternative to Shortcut #66: Ctrl + F4, which closes the Excel program.

Shortcut #98: Ctrl + X

This will cut the contents of an active cell. When you say "cut", it will remove the data in a cell and will place it temporarily in the Clipboard so that you can paste the contents in another cell.

Shortcut #99: Ctrl + Y

The Ctrl + Y shortcut runs the Redo function, which means that it will repeat the previous command that you have done.

Shortcut #100: Ctrl + Z

Lastly, Ctrl + Z serve as the shortcut for the Undo function. This will reverse your latest command in Excel.

And that finishes our countdown for the Top 100 keyboard shortcuts in Microsoft Excel. To wrap things up, the last chapter will provide some pointers in "memorizing" these shortcuts the easiest way.

Chapter 6: Pointers for the Excel Novice

Most people will most likely feel daunted with the mere volume of shortcuts in this book. "How can I ever memorize a hundred of these combinations?", says most people. This fear of memorization only impedes the learning process. As such, you should stay away from this negative thinking.

Practice a Couple of Shortcuts Every Week

To be able to remember these shortcuts effectively, you should use them as often as you could. Have this book by your side always so that you will have a guide as you try to absorb each of these shortcuts. Better yet, you can jot down a couple of shortcuts in a small list so that you can try some of these tricks in your school or the office.

After finishing let's say at least five shortcuts for a week, add another five in the succeeding weeks. Just don't forget the previous shortcuts that you have learned. In no time, you will be able to use these keyboard combinations without the help of a cheat sheet.

Don't Use the Numeric Keypad

Although most people on the go use laptops such as students, many people still use the full-sized keyboard that has a built-in numeric keypad at the right side.

Although several characters in the listed shortcuts are there, the Microsoft Excel does not recognize the use of numeric keypad in its shortcuts. As such, you shouldn't try to practice these shortcuts via the numeric keypad; just use the main keyboard itself.

That ends all the pointers in this guide for Excel shortcuts. With that, you should apply all the learnings that you have discovered through this book in your daily Excel tasks. Hopefully, you'll be a more efficient Excel user as you incorporate these shortcuts in using the said spreadsheet program.

Conclusion

Thank you again for purchasing this book!

I hope this book was able to help you to learn the secrets behind mastering Microsoft Excel, which are the 100 keyboard shortcuts.

The next step is to make use of these shortcuts every time you operate on the Excel application. Through this, you can now easily work on your Excel spreadsheets with only a minimal use of a mouse.

Finally, if you enjoyed this book, please take the time to share your thoughts and post a review on Amazon. We do our best to reach out to readers and provide the best value we can. Your positive review will help us achieve that. It'd be greatly appreciated!

Thank you and good luck!

Book 2
JavaScript Professional
Programming Made Easy
BY SAM KEY

Expert JavaScripts Programming
Language Success in a Day for Any
Computer User!

Table Of Contents

Introduction

I want to thank you and congratulate you for purchasing the book, "Professional JavaScript Programming Made Easy: Expert JavaScripts Programming Language Success In A Day for Any Computer User!"

This book contains proven steps and strategies on how to code JavaScript from scratch.

This book will give you a solid idea on how JavaScript works and how it can be applied to your web pages. This is an ideal book that every beginner should read. However, it is required that you already know HTML and CSS.

Familiarity with other programming languages such as Java, Visual Basic, and C is a plus since it will make it easier for you to learn and understand the concepts behind the processes involved in coding JavaScript.

Every explanation in the book will be accompanied by an example. Those examples will be shown in Courier New font; in case that font is not available, it will be shown in a monospaced generic family font instead.

To learn and code JavaScript, all you need is a text editing tool such as Notepad in Windows or TextEdit in Macintosh computers. However, it is recommend that you use a source code editor or a text editing tool with syntax highlighting that supports HTML, CSS, and JavaScript languages to speed up your learning and reduce the typos you will make.

One of the best and free source code editor tools you can get from the internet is Notepad++. It will be discussed in the last chapter of the book.

Thanks again for purchasing this book, I hope you enjoy it!

Chapter 1: Introduction to JavaScript

JavaScript is a scripting or programming language that is mainly used for web pages. Almost all websites use it to provide their visitors a richer browsing experience. Compared to coding HTML, JavaScript is real programming.

It is safe to say that JavaScript is the most popular and most widely used programming language in the world. JavaScript is easy to learn, and that is why web developers or even hobbyists can use it after a few days of studying it.

Unlike other programming languages, JavaScript is easy to learn and apply practically. The programs or scripts created from JavaScript are used by millions of people – even though they do not know they are already using them.

JavaScript can turn your old HTML files, which are static, into dynamic. You can embed JavaScript into your files for you to deliver web pages with dynamic content and appearance.

To embed JavaScript to your HTML file, you must enclose your script inside script HTML tags (<script></script>). Commonly, you should place the script tags inside the head HTML tags (<head></head>). However, there will be times that you might want or need to place them inside your page's body (<body></body>).

On the other hand, JavaScript can be placed in an external file and linked on a web page to work. It will be considered to be a part of the HTML file being parsed by the browser once it is linked.

Client and Server Side Scripting

In web development, JavaScript is termed as a client side scripting language. All the scripts that you write in JavaScript are executed on the client side, which is your or your visitors' browser.

On the other hand, PHP and ASP are server side scripting languages. As you might have guessed, the scripts or programs created using those two are executed on the server and their results are usually sent to the client.

Programming Box Set #70: Excel Shortcuts & JavaScript Professional Programming Made Easy

The two complete the concept of DHTML (Dynamic HTML). When you use client and server side scripting, your pages will become more dynamic and interactive. With them, you can create social media websites, online games, and even your own search engine. And those statements are not exaggerated. You are truly a few steps away from greatness once you master JavaScript and a server side scripting language.

However, take note that learning client side scripting is a prerequisite before learning server side scripting. After all, most of the functions and features that you will create using server side scripting will require or need the support of client side scripting. Also, client side scripting is a good introduction to programming for web developers who have no experience or even any idea on how programming works.

Before you start learning and applying JavaScript to your web documents, you should learn and master HTML and CSS. In JavaScript, you will be mostly dealing with HTML elements, so it is a requirement that you know about HTML elements and attributes.

Alternatively, if you want to use JavaScript to perform advanced styling on your document such as animations and dynamic layouts, then you should have a solid background on CSS.

To give you a short summary of the relationship between HTML, CSS, and JavaScript, take note of these pointers:

- HTML is used to define the content and elements of your web page.

- CSS is used to specify or precisely define the appearance and layout of your web page.

- JavaScript is used to create functionalities in your web page. It can also be used to define content like HTML and define appearances like CSS.

With JavaScript, you can fully control everything on your web page. You can change an HTML element's content. For example, you can change the text content of a paragraph element with JavaScript.

You can also change the value of one of the attributes of an HTML element. For example, you can change the HREF attribute of a link you inserted on your document.

And lastly, you can change the CSS or styling values of an HTML element. For example, you can change the font-weight of one of your headers in your web document with JavaScript, too.

Also, with JavaScript, you have full control on when it will be applied, unlike CSS. You can run your scripts before the page loads, while the page is loading, after the page loaded, and while your user browses the page.

On the other hand, you can make those changes automatic or triggered by the visitor. You can add other factors such as time of the day, specific user actions, or user browsing behavior to trigger those changes or functions.

Chapter 2: HTML DOM and Assigning Values

How can JavaScript do all of that? It can do all of that because it takes advantage of the HTML DOM or Document Object Model. JavaScript can access, modify, and remove any HTML element together with its properties by using HTML DOM.

Assigning Attribute Values with JavaScript

With CSS, you have dealt with selectors. By using the right selector, you can change the CSS style of a specific element, group or class of elements, group of similar elements, handpicked elements, or all of the elements in your page. By this point, you must already know how id's and classes works.

JavaScript almost works like that, too. To change the content of an element, value of an element's property or attribute, or style of an element, you will need to select them first and assign a value. Below is an example of using JavaScript to change a paragraph element's (which has a value of "testparagraph" for its id attribute) font size:

```
<head>
<script>
document.getElementById("testparagraph"
).style.fontSize = "17px";
</script>
</head>
<body>
<p id='testparagraph' >This a paragraph. This is
another sentence. This is the last sentence.</p>
</body>
```

The previous line's equivalent to CSS is:

#testparagraph {font-size: 17px;}

They have different syntax, but they will have the same result. In the CSS example, the paragraph with the "testparagraph" id was selected by placing a pound sign and typing the id value.

In JavaScript, "testparagraph" was selected using DOM. If you will translate the example JavaScript line to plain English, the line says to the browser that the line of code pertains to something or will do something within the document, which is your webpage.

Then the next part tells the browser that you are looking for a certain element that has a value of "testparagraph" on its id attribute. The next part tells the browser that you will do something to the style attribute of the "testparagraph" element. And the last part tells the browser that you will assign a value on the fontSize within the element's style attribute.

In JavaScript, the equals sign (=) means that you will assign a value to the variable or property on its left. And the value that you will assign on the variable or property is on the right.

On the example, you will assign the value "17px" to the fontSize style attribute of the element "testparagraph" that is located within your HTML document. The semicolon at the end tells the browser that it is the end of the line for that code, and it should parse the next line for it to execute.

Browser Parsing Behavior

By default, that previous JavaScript example will not work. The reason is that browsers read and execute HTML documents line by line – from the starting tag of the html tag, the browser will perform scripts, apply CSS values, place the HTML elements, place their specific contents, etcetera, until the browser reach the closing html tag.

In the example, the line asks the browser for an element that has the value "testparagraph" in its id attribute in the document. Unfortunately, the browser has not reached the body of the document where the definition of the element "testparagraph" resides.

Because of that, the browser will return an error saying that there is no element that has that attribute. You cannot assign a value for the attribute font size style to a nonexistent or null object. Hence, when the browser reaches the definition of the element "testparagraph", its font size will not be changed to the value you have set in the JavaScript code.

The solution to that is simple: you can place the script after the part where the element "testparagraph" was defined, and that is any location after the closing paragraph of the element "testparagraph".

Chapter 3: JavaScript Statements

In the last part of the previous chapter, the book loosely discussed about how browsers read HTML files and JavaScript lines and how you can assign values to an attribute. This chapter will supplement you with further discussions about that and JavaScript statements.

To construct a program using a programming language, you will need to write lines of codes. Those lines of codes are called statements. A statement is a line of code that contains an instruction for the computer to execute. In JavaScript, the one that executes the code is your internet browser.

Statements in JavaScript might contain the following: Keywords, Expressions, Operators, Comments, and Values. Below are sample lines of JavaScript that this chapter will dissect; this is done so that you will know the parts that comprise JavaScript statements:

var x; // This is a comment line.
var y; // To create one, you must place two forward slashes.
var z; // Comment lines are ignored by the browser.
x = 1 + 1; // So you can place them before or after a statement.
y = "Hello World." // And it will not affect the syntax.
z = 10 // But do not put them in the middle of a statement.
Keywords

In the example, the word var is a keyword. Typically, keywords are reserved words that you cannot use in your program except when you need to use their purpose. In the sample statements, the keyword var tells the browser to create a variable named x. Variables will be discussed later.

Expressions

On the other hand, 1 + 1 is an expression and the + and = sign are examples of operators. Expressions, in computer programming, are combinations of operators, values, constants, and variables that will be interpreted by the computer to produce a result. In x = 1 + 1, the browser will compute or evaluate that expression and return a value of 2. Expressions are not limited to arithmetic operations in JavaScript. Expressions can be in form of Boolean comparison, string operations, and etcetera.

Values

There are two values types that you will see and use in JavaScript. The first type is fixed or literal values; the second type is variables.

Literal Values

Numbers, Strings (text enclosed in single or double quotes), and even Expressions are literal values. In the example, the parts "Hello World" (string), 10 (number), and 1 + 1 (expression) are literal values.

Variables

On the other hand, variables are data containers. Variables can contain literal values such as strings, numbers, arrays, expressions, and even objects.

To use or create one, you must name it or create an identifier for it. Identifiers are combinations of letters, underscores, and dollar signs and must not be the same with any keywords or reserved words in JavaScript.

However, take note that identifiers must start with a letter, an underscore, or a dollar sign only. Starting with a number will return an error, and including symbols other than underscores and dollar signs will not be accepted by JavaScript.

Local Variable and Global Variables

There are two types of variables in JavaScript. The first one is local and the second one is global. The type of variable depends on where it was declared. The difference between them is how they are handled in the script.

Variables that are declared outside of functions will become a global variable. And variables that are declared inside functions will become a local variable.

Global variables will stay on the memory until the web page is closed. It can be referenced and used anywhere in the script. On the other hand, local variables will only stay on the memory until the browser finishes executing the function where the variable was declared. It can be only referenced and used by the function where it was declared. Functions will be discussed later in this book.

In the sample JavaScript statements, the letters x, y, and z are global variables.

To create a variable in JavaScript, you must use the var keyword – just like in the previous example. To assign values to them, you can use the equal operator.

Operators

There are multiple of operators that you can use in JavaScript. And it can be categorized into the following:

- Arithmetic
- Assignment
- String
- Comparison
- Logical
- Conditional
- Bitwise
- Typeof
- Delete Unary +

Only the first four types of operators are mostly the ones that you will frequently use during your early days of JavaScript programming: Arithmetic, Assignment, String, and Comparison. The remaining operators are typically used for advanced projects and might be confusing for beginners.

On the other hand, take note that some of the operator symbols may serve two purposes or more. For example, the + sign can be used as an arithmetic, string, or unary + operator depending on the condition or your goal.

Comments

You might already have an idea on what comments are. As mentioned before, they are ignored by browsers, and their only function is to serve as reminders or notes for you – just like the comments in HTML. You can create a new line of comment by using two forward slashes. If you want to create a block of comment, start it with /* and end it with */.

Chapter 4: JavaScript's Basic Syntax

For the browser to execute a JavaScript statement, the statement must follow the correct syntax and must only have one instruction (this may vary depending the code).

Just a small mistake in the syntax will make the computer do something different from what you want to happen or it might not do nothing and return an error.

If you have a large block of code and one of the statements gets an error, the browser will not execute the lines that follow the statement that generated an error.

Due to that, it is important that you always check your code and avoid creating mistakes to make sure that you will achieve the things you want to happen with JavaScript.

JavaScript Syntax

JavaScript, just like other computer languages, follow syntax. In computer programming, syntax is a set of rules that you must follow when writing codes.

One of the syntax rules in JavaScript is to terminate each statement with a colon. It is like placing a dot in every sentence you make.

This rule is flexible due to ASI (Automatic Semicolon Inserting). Even if you do not place a semicolon at the end of your statement, once you start a new line, the previous line will be considered as a complete statement – as if it has a semicolon at the end. However, not placing semicolons is bad practice since it might produce bugs and errors.

Another rule is to make sure that you close brackets, parentheses, and quotations in your code. For example, leaving a dangling curly brace will result in an error. And with quotation marks, if you started with a single quote, end it with a single quote. If you start with a double quote, end with a double quote.

Take note that JavaScript is a case-sensitive language. Unlike HTML wherein you can use lower, upper, and mixed case on tags and attributes, JavaScript will return an error once you use the wrong case for a method or variable. For example, changing the capitalization of the letter b in the getElementById will result to an error.

Never create variables that have the similar name with keywords or reserved words. Also, always declare variables. If you do not explicitly declare them and use them on your statements, you might get unexpected results or a reference error. For example:

var y;

var z;

y = 1;

z = 1 + x;

Once your browser reads the last line, no value will be assigned to z because the browser will return a reference error.

That is just a few of the rules in JavaScript's syntax. Some methods and keywords follow certain syntax. Remember them to prevent yourself from the hassle of unneeded debugging.

Chapter 5: Functions and Events

You already know by now what statements are and how to write statements in accordance to JavaScript's syntax rules. You also know how to assign values to an HTML element's attribute by using JavaScript. In this chapter, you will know how to create functions or methods.

A function is a block of statements that you can call or invoke anytime to execute. In other programming languages, functions are called subroutines, methods, or procedures. The statements inside a function will not be immediately executed when the browser parses the HTML document. It will only run or be executed if it is called or invoked.

Purposes of Functions

What are the purposes of functions? First, it allows you to control when to execute a block of statements as explained previously.

Second, it allows you to create 'mini' programs in your script. For example, if you want to make a paragraph to be centered align, to have a heavier font, and to have a bigger font size when you click the paragraph, you can create a function for that goal and capture an event that will trigger that function once you click on the paragraph.

Third, creating functions is a good way to separate lengthy blocks of statements into smaller chunks. Maintaining and debugging your script will be much easier with functions.

Fourth, it can effectively lessen redundancy in your script. Instead of writing the same sequence of statements repeatedly in your script, you can just create a function, and just call it again when you need the browser to execute the statements within it once more.

Creating Functions

To create a function, you will need to use the keyword function. When you create a function you must follow a simple syntax. Below is an example of a function:

function MakeBolderAndBigger(elementID) {

```
document.getElementById(elementID).style.fontSiz
e = "20px";
document.getElementById(elementID).style.fontWe
ight = "20px";
}
```

In the example, the keyword function was followed with MakeBolderAndBigger. That part is the function's name. Naming a function has the same rules with naming a variable identifier.

After the function's name, there is elementID which is enclosed in parentheses. That part of the function is called a parameter. You can place as many parameters that you want or none at all. If you place multiple parameters, you must separate them with a comma and a space. If you are not going to use parameters, just leave it blank but never forget to place the parentheses.

A parameter stores that value or the function arguments that was placed on it when the function is invoked. That parameter will act as local variable in the function. This part will be discussed further later.

Then, after the parameter, you will see a curly brace. And after the statements, there is another curly brace.

The first brace act as a sign that tells the browsers that any statements following it is a code block for the function. The second brace tells the browsers that the code block is finished, and any line of code after it is not related to the function. Those are the rules you need to follow when creating a function.

Invoking Functions

There are two common ways to invoke a function. First, you can invoke it within your script. Second, you can invoke it by placing and triggering event handlers.

Invoke within Code

The first method of invoking functions is easy. All you need to do is to type the name of the function, and fill in the arguments that the function's parameters require. To invoke the example function using the first method, you can simply type this:

MakeBolderAndBigger("testparagraph");

Once your browser reads that, it will process the function. Since you have placed "testparagraph" as the argument for the parameter elementID, elementID will have a value of "testparagraph". It will now act as a variable.

When the browser executes the first statement in the function, which is document.getElementById(elementID).style.fontSize = "20px";, it will select the element "testparagraph" and change its font size value to 20px.

On the other hand, you can actually provide no argument for function parameters. If you do this instead:

MakeBolderAndBigger();

The browser will execute the function. However, since you did not store any value to the parameter, the parameter elementID will be undefined and will have the value undefined.

Because of that, when the first statement tries to look for the element with the id attribute of elementID, which has the value of undefined, it will return an error.

Once the browser finishes executing the function, it will return on reading the next line of code after the function invocation. For example:

MakeBolderAndBigger("testparagraph"); document.getElementById("testparagraph").style.c olor = "blue";

After the browser finishes executing the function MakeBolderAndBigger, it will proceed on executing the next statement below and make the font color of "testparagraph" to blue. The example above is the same as coding:

document.getElementById("testparagraph").style.fontSize = "20px"; document.getElementById("testparagraph").style.fontWeight = "20px"; document.getElementById("testparagraph").style.color = "blue";

Invoke with Events

Every action that a user does in a web page and every action that the browser performs are considered events. A few of those events are:

- When the page finishes loading

- When a user or script changes the content of a text field

- When a user click a button or an HTML element

- When a user presses on a keyboard key

To invoke a function when an event happens, you must tell the browser by placing some piece of codes in your page's HTML. Below is an example:

<button onClick='MakeBolderAndBigger("testparagraph");' >Invoke Function</button>

When a user clicks on that button element, it will trigger the function MakeBolderAndBigger. The syntax for that is simple. Just insert the event inside the opening tag of an HTML element that has the event that you want to capture, place an equal sign, place the function that you want to execute together with the arguments you need to place on it, and then enclose the function in quotes.

By the way, be wary of quotes. If you used a single quote to enclose the function, then use double quotes to enclose the values on your arguments. Just think of it as if you are assigning values on an element's style attribute in HTML. Also, as best practice, never forget to place a semicolon at the end.

As a reference, below are some of the events that you can use in HTML and JavaScript:

- onClick – triggers when the user clicks on the HTML element

- onMouseOver – triggers when the user hovers on the HTML element

- onMouseOut – triggers when the user's mouse pointers move out from the element's display

- onKeyDown – triggers when the user presses a keyboard key

- onChange – triggers when the user changes the content of a text field

- onLoad – triggers when the browser is done loading the body, images, frames, and other scripts

Chapter 6: Debugging, Text Editing Tool, and References

In modern browsers, most of JavaScript errors are handled automatically and ignored to prevent browsing disruption. So when testing your scripts when opening your HTML files on a browser, it is difficult to spot errors and debug.

Web Developer Consoles on Browsers

Fortunately, a few of those browsers have built-in developer consoles where you can monitor errors and the resources that your page generates and uses. One of those browsers that have this functionality is Google Chrome. To access its developer console, you can press F12 on your keyboard while a page is open on it.

Pressing the key will open the developer tools panel within Chrome, and you can click on the Console tab to monitor the errors that your page generates. Aside from monitoring errors, you can use it to test statements, check the values of your variables, call functions, etc.

Text Editing Tool with Syntax Highlighting

You can get away with a few problems when writing HTML and CSS on typical text editing tools like Notepad. However, with JavaScript coding, using those ordinary tools is a challenge. Unlike the two, JavaScript has a strict and vast syntax. Just one typo in your script and you will start hunting bugs after you test the statements you wrote. After all, it is a programming language unlike HTML which is a markup language.

To make your life easier, it is best that you use a text editing tool with syntax highlighting when coding JavaScript. One of the best tools out there on the Web is Notepad++. It is free and it is as lightweight (in terms of resource usage) and as simple as Notepad.

The syntax highlighting will help you spot missing brackets and quotation marks. It will also prevent you from using keywords as variables since keywords are automatically highlighted in a different color, which will help you realize sooner that they are identifiers you cannot use for variables.

References

As of now, you have only learned the basics of how to code JavaScript. You might have been itching to change the values of other attributes in your HTML code, but you do not know the HTML DOM to use. On the other hand, you might be interested on knowing the other operators that you can use in your script.

The book has omitted most of them since it focused more on the coding process in JavaScript. Thankfully, you can just look up those values and operators on the net. To give you a head start, this a link to the JavaScript reference list made by the developers in the Mozilla Foundation: https://developer.mozilla.org/en-US/docs/Web/JavaScript/Reference.

Conclusion

Thank you again for purchasing this book!

I hope this book was able to help you to learn the basics of coding with JavaScript.

The next step is to:

Master the HTML DOM.

Become familiar with other keywords and their usage.

Finally, if you enjoyed this book, please take the time to share your thoughts and post a review on Amazon. We do our best to reach out to readers and provide the best value we can. Your positive review will help us achieve that. It'd be greatly appreciated!

Thank you and good luck!

Check Out My Other Books

Below you'll find some of my other popular books that are popular on Amazon and Kindle as well. Simply click on the links below to check them out. Alternatively, you can visit my author page on Amazon to see other work done by me.

C Programming Success in a Day

Android Programming in a Day

C ++ Programming Success in a Day

C Programming Professional Made Easy

Python Programming in a Day

PHP Programming Professional Made Easy

HTML Professional Programming Made Easy

CSS Programming Professional Made Easy

Windows 8 Tips for Beginners

Programming Box Set #70: Excel Shortcuts & JavaScript Professional Programming Made Easy

If the links do not work, for whatever reason, you can simply search for these titles on the Amazon website to find them.